Portrait of Dylan

A Photographer's Memoir by Rollie McKenna

Introduction by John Malcolm Brinnin

First published in the United States of America 1982 by
Stemmer House Publishers, Inc.
First published in Great Britain 1982 by J. M. Dent &
Sons Ltd.

A Barbara Holdridge book

Printed in the United States of America
for
J. M. Dent & Sons Ltd.
Aldine House, Welbeck Street, London W1

ISBN 0-460-04573-3

Acknowledgments

The author and publishers are grateful to the following for permission to reprint copyright material:
The Trustees for the Copyrights of the late Dylan Thomas for all quotations from the works of Dylan Thomas;
Atlantic-Little, Brown (Boston) for the quotation from *Dylan Thomas in America,* copyright © 1955 by John Malcolm Brinnin;
David Higham Associates for the quotation from *Leftover Life to Kill,* © 1957 by Caitlin Thomas.

To Pat
and her children,
Gini, Freer, Vicki and Pud

Introduction

A photographer who can bring a twinkle to the apostolic eyes of T. S. Eliot, catch Robert Frost as the sage of woodlands wild and, from the aging W. H. Auden, evoke the look of a startled faun, is obviously one able to command many kinds of attention. How Rollie McKenna does it remains a secret, perhaps even to herself. Yet it's clear that she is not to be counted among those photographers who trick their subjects into morbid caricature, and certainly not among those who try to efface themselves in order to become mere mechanical adjuncts to an instrument. Her presence in what emerges from the darkroom is as palpable as it is in the living room or any other room where, disarming her subjects with easy chatter, bird-like interjections and firm but gentle instructions, she lifts a camera and, without interrupting her monologue, presses the shutter.

This presence is a personality not easy to define, a balance of contraries—of humane perception and aesthetic strictness; of a bent for the large design and a belief in the resonance of the minute particular; of a conservative disposition entirely open to the boldest manifestations of eccentricity and latter-day bohemianism. Sensing this, subjects of whatever temperament or persuasion respond to the photographer herself with an interest so keen as to make the camera in her hand a negligible distraction. The result is a kind of diverted ease in expressions everywhere evident in her grand gallery of mid-century poets—among whom Dylan Thomas was one of the youngest and, in his brief term, the most celebrated.

I first met Thomas in January 1950, when, arriving in New York at my invitation, he stepped from a now archaic Constellation into the customs shed of the airport called Idlewild that is now named Kennedy. I first met Rollie at sea in August of the same year, aboard the *S.S. Liberté*. I was on my way to visit Dylan in London; Rollie's destination was Italy, there to add to an already brilliant series of architectural photographs new ones of the Ghiberti doors in Florence and the basilica domes of San Marco in Venice. By the time Dylan came back to America in 1952, she and I were close friends and working partners in a project to provide the Poetry Center of New York's YM-YWHA—of which I was Director—with a comprehensive collection of photographs of those poets the Center had begun to present. Dylan's wife Caitlin accompanied him on this second American visit and the first snow-bright days of it found us all together at Rollie's house in Millbrook, New York. There she took some of the pictures by which Dylan is best remembered—the poet "crucified" in serpentine branches of wisteria; reclining on a mound of straw in what seems like pastoral languor when, actually, the temperature hovered around zero; and (the photograph of Dylan which Dame Edith Sitwell preferred above all others) standing tall in his heavy tweeds while bright sun broadens his shy smile. As I watched Rollie at work on this occasion I was able to confirm for myself what, on other occasions, I had merely sensed: that her remarkable portraits are the product of an active cooperation between the photographer and her subject in a state of rapport achieved almost instantly. Sometimes choosing his own settings and almost always "acting" for the camera, Dylan was enough of a professional to want good photographs. Yet, I could tell by his good-humored patience and self-deprecating repartee that, just as much, he wanted to please Rollie.

So began a friendship between them that made possible a photographic record of Dylan's last years unique in its opportunities and unmatched in its range and variety. The image of Dylan the public man, pouter-pigeon bold on stage in his blue suit and polka-dot bow-tie, is balanced by Dylan the shy and uneasy *paterfamilias* in a grey flannel shirt, his forehead scarred by just one of the falls—from grace and sobriety—that would lead to his early death. The tawdry commercial streets of the edges of Greenwich Village, contrasted with the green-hedged lanes of the village of Laugharne, tell that part of Dylan's story which he himself was never able to resolve. The pensive Dylan and the raucous Dylan are here, and so are the searching eyes of a man of genius and the lurking mischief of a little boy trying to be bad.

My own favorite is the most familiar—Dylan in shirtsleeves, a cigarette dangling from his lip, as he instructs the cast of *Under Milk Wood* to "love the words, *love* the words." (The shirt was one of half a dozen I'd bought for him—partly in the hope that he'd give up his habit of purloining other shirts from hosts like the Attorney General of the United States, and partly in the hope that, as owner of shirts of quality and long life, he'd at last consider laundering a reasonable alternative to jettisoning). This is the rare Dylan—a man absorbed in the demands of his own authority, every gesture urging his actors toward that clarity of utterance which was always his foremost goal.

"The camera never lies," it is said. "One picture is worth a thousand words." These clichés have a nice ring to them but nobody, at least nowadays, finds either credible. Yet I cannot lightly put aside a suspicion, based on my own fleeting appearance in this pictorial record, that neither assertion can finally be dismissed. I had come to Laugharne to dissuade Dylan from making another American tour; he had welcomed me in the belief, generous but mistaken, that I alone could make another American visit possible. Angry and fearful, Caitlin was indifferent to my "position," if indeed she grasped it, and to Dylan's rosy expectations of a vast haul of American dollars for comparatively few public appearances. And there, under Rollie's observant eye, we are—three people each in our own way troubled, oblivious to the camera, caught up in a circumstance too tangled to undo until, days later, Dylan would pull the first crucial string and so set out upon a journey from which he would not return.

Sometimes unflinching in its revelations, this book is a documentary statement unhurriedly composed at a time in Dylan Thomas's life no one then believed would be the only time. Rollie McKenna's words modestly rehearse the association that made it possible and her pictures vividly recall what time has begun to darken. She has worked, then and now, to tell a truth with all the resourcefulness that characterizes her professional approach, perhaps unaware that, in the process, an essentially reportorial account has been transformed into a loving tribute.

John Malcolm Brinnin
Cambridge, Massachusetts
February 1982

The wide flats of the estuary are filling rapidly. Constantly changing, curling ribbons of water spread themselves out on the sands below the Boathouse, to which I have come from the village along the narrow Cliff Walk. I stand there looking for a sign of Caitlin Thomas.

Slowly, a heavy, dirty-white rowboat approaches. In it are three people —Caitlin and, as I will in a few seconds learn, her daughter Aeron and her eldest son Llewelyn—and a dog. I wave, and Caitlin, smiling, returns my greeting. The dog's name is Mably, and they have all gone on a picnic, stopping to gather cockles in the muddy sands of the river Taf.

"It turned away from the
blithe country
And down the other air
and the blue altered
sky
Streamed again a wonder
of summer
With apples
Pears and red currants
And I saw in the turning
so clearly a child's
Forgotten mornings when
he walked with his
mother
Through the parables
Of sun light
And the legends of the
green chapels . . ."

"My own news is very big and simple. I was married three days ago; to Caitlin Macnamara; in Penzance registry office; with no money, no prospect of money, no attendant friends or relatives, and in complete happiness. We've been meaning to from the first day we met, and now we are free and glad. . . ."

So begins, in the late summer of 1953, the first of my two visits in this year to Laugharne, Carmarthenshire, in southwest Wales. Here Dylan Thomas has spent most of the last fifteen years of his life with Caitlin and their three children, the third of whom is Colm, four years old. In barely two months, Dylan will die in a New York hospital, leaving Caitlin's and the children's lives split into pieces at the very moment when the celebration of Wales's greatest lyric poet is to begin. His poems will resound throughout the English-speaking world and eventually win him a plaque in Westminster Abbey.

But all of this is in the future.

Dylan, Caitlin tells me, is due back tonight from a reading tour of north Wales, in the course of which he will also appear on television. Waiting for his return, Caitlin and I—having met only once before in America, and a little uneasy with one another—seek ways to become reacquainted.

We walk in the light-dappled woods nearby, play with the children and Mably on the muddy beach, and perform chores on the wooden balcony of the Boathouse, their home. Dolly, a maid of all work, washes the dishes, polishes the children's shoes and helps Caitlin brush the tangles out of Aeron's thick auburn hair, as I photograph everything my senses can absorb.

In the atmosphere of easy domesticity in Caitlin's own house, I sense that she is beginning to like me, despite her distrust of Americans in general. To her the United States is where Dylan drinks excessively and "wastes" himself in work that has nothing to do with creativity. It is the country where he is lionized by a literary public and sought after by women; and from which, despite his successful reading engagements, he usually returns to her with not much more money than he had when he left.

"In my seashaken house on a breakneck of rocks . . ."

That night we view Dylan's television performance in the small kitchen of Browns Hotel, Dylan's favorite pub, where we are joined by his mother, Florence, and the proprietors of the hotel, Ivy and Ebie Williams, as well as other friends of the Thomases. Dylan has chosen to read "A Story": "If you can call it a story. There's no real beginning or end and there's very little in the middle. It is all about a day's outing, by charabanc, to Porthcawl, which, of course, the charabanc never reached, and it happened when I was so high and much nicer." One of the points of this reminiscence is a boy's enchanted recognition that life itself might be an endless pub crawl. "The Blue Bull, the Dragon, the Star of Wales, the Twll in the Wall, the Sour Grapes, the Shepherd's Arms, the Bells of Aberdovey: I had nothing to do in the whole wild August world but remember the names where the outing stopped and keep an eye on the charabanc. . . ."

As Dylan reads, everyone is talking quietly and laughing approvingly. This is the man they know, not the celebrated stranger who from time to time mysteriously steals off to far-away America. The escapades of his companions on this fictional pub crawl bear unmistakable, and slightly uncomfortable, resemblances to Dylan's own behavior as a grown-up.

"Shall I unbolt or stay
Alone till the day I die
Unseen by stranger-eyes
In this white house?
Hands, hold you poison
or grapes?"

Next morning I meet him at the Boathouse. Greeting me affably and, I think, a bit shyly, he is the same round, rumple-shirted man I knew in America. But I cannot help observing that his face is bloated, his expression worried, haunted, and that over his eye is a deep and freshly scabbed cut.

"I'm glad to see you," he says. "Isn't John with you?" John will arrive in a few days, I tell him. "Sorry the old sod isn't here now," he replies.

John Malcolm Brinnin, director of New York's YM-YWHA Poetry Center, had been responsible for bringing Dylan to the United States three years earlier. After the brilliant first performance of the play *Under Milk Wood* at the Center, John and I had accepted a commission by the managing editor of *Mademoiselle* to do a story about Dylan's daily life in Laugharne and the surrounding countryside. Since, at the moment, Dylan neither looks nor feels photogenic, he and I decide to postpone picture-taking until our friend is on the scene. I go off to London, and ten days later drive back to Laugharne, accompanied by John.

This time Dylan's mother asks me to stay with her in the Pelican, her small tidy home across the street from Browns Hotel. She keeps a fat cat, and a low fire in the hearth—partly for the cat and partly to keep out the chilly dampness that creeps into stucco houses in seaside towns. The parlor, which contains Dylan's books and those of his father, seems to be almost hermetically sealed.

Death, I soon learn, is no stranger to Florence Thomas. Within this year she has lost not only her husband but her daughter, Dylan's sister Nancy. For further tribulation, she has broken her leg and now walks with two canes. Nonetheless, she is cheerful and hospitable. Concerned about Dylan's health, she is also perplexed by what she regards as his and Caitlin's disorderly way of life. She finds solace in the grandchildren, who are frequent visitors to the Pelican, especially Aeron, who often snuggles in bed with this motherly white-haired woman.

John has stayed in Llewelyn's room at the Boathouse. Meeting early at a sidewalk bench near the post office, we make plans for the day. Dylan still is not looking very well when he joins us to stroll through the winding streets, to peer into flyblown and fading shop windows, to greet passersby who view my large lens and camera with obvious trepidation, and to linger before yellow-washed "Sea View" and other houses in which he and Caitlin lived in the early years of their marriage. We are delighted with the colored stone, glass and tile insets surrounding the windows of some of the houses. On a side street, we stop to watch children in cardboard military hats, playing war games with broomstick handles. We wander past Laugharne Castle to a marshy area where little boys climb over disintegrating boats, and come to the path that leads to Sir John's hill. Turning around, we can see, above a great pile of cockle shells, the whole village and its castle.

W E

RETURN

"Outside, the sun springs down on the rough and tumbling town."

"And in the town, the shops squeak open."

". . . where everything is sold: custard, buckets, henna, rat-traps, shrimp-nets, sugar, stamps, confetti, paraffin, hatchets, whistles."

This undistinguished medieval ruin is, at this time, in the care of Richard Hughes, author of *A High Wind in Jamaica,* who lived in the nearby pink-washed cottage. There, as his guest, Dylan had courted another guest, Caitlin, some fifteen years earlier. The castle itself is a shambles, but accessible by permission. Those brave enough scale ladders to its crumbling heights for the spectacular seaward view over the rooftops of the village. The only "human" in the decaying garden is the vaguely regal bust of a woman who seems to be guarding a lost domain.

The pubs will soon be open, Dylan reminds us; but we still have time to walk below the clock tower past Browns and on through the Lychgate to the parish church of St. Martin. This stone structure, said to be founded on the remains of a Druid temple, stands in a deep grove of ancient trees. Its adjoining cemetery, heavily shaded, is cool and dank. Headstones have been pushed askew by tree roots; vines, bracken and lichen are so thick that one has to look closely to distinguish familiar Welsh names like Jones, Williams and Morgan. I see no bats, but bats must certainly live there.

"Hoo, there, in castle keep,
You king singsong
owls . . ."

"The owls are hunting. Look, over Bethesda gravestones one hoots and swoops and catches a mouse . . ."

"... The ship's clock in the bar says half past eleven. Half past eleven is opening time. The hands of the clock have stayed still at half past eleven for fifty years. It is always opening time in The Sailor's Arms."

When the pubs open, Dylan is ready for Browns, a pint or two of bitter, and a game of "nap" (Napoleon). This supposedly simple four-handed card game, with bids, trumps and tricks, defies my understanding. When Dylan is in the village, I learn, he plays a more or less continuous round with Ivy and Ebie and Ebie's brother Billy. Are the stakes another pint of ale?

On the way to the Boathouse for lunch, we stop at Dylan's study, a faded green shack overlooking the estuary. Once inside the low-arched, wooden door, we can see that it is sparsely furnished; a writing table, a bookcase, a straight wooden chair and an iron stove, which to this day has not been lit, simply because it has no chimney. Books and manuscripts, old bottles of dried ink, pens and bits of paper, spent matches and empty Woodbine packets lie on the desk. Spiders and their webs compete with ivy to occupy the empty spaces. I am flattered to see my photograph of W. H. Auden, which I'd given Dylan in New York, pinned to the whitewashed wall. But the place of honor, just above the writing table, belongs to the bearded Walt Whitman. Elsewhere are Marianne Moore, D. H. Lawrence, Breughel's dancing villagers, a Chagall and other reproductions clipped from magazines.

"... for a whole year I have been able to write nothing, nothing, nothing at all but one tangled, sentimental poem as preface to a collection of poems written years ago."

"Pale rain over the
dwindling harbour
And over the sea wet
church the size of a snail
With its horns through
mist . . ."

Dylan's view from his desk looks to the south where

> Over Sir John's hill,
> The hawk on fire hangs still;
>
> . . .
>
> Where the elegiac fisherbird stabs and paddles
> In the pebbly dab-filled
> Shallow and sedge, "dilly dilly" calls the loft hawk,
> "Come and be killed . . ."

To the east, in Llanybri across the Taf, he can see the spired little church about which he has written, "Pale rain over the dwindling harbour/ and over the sea wet church the size of a snail/with its horns through mist . . ."

"... so that I can get down to those ogre words again without nightmares of doubt and debt, and my dear diabolic family shall be protected for a time."

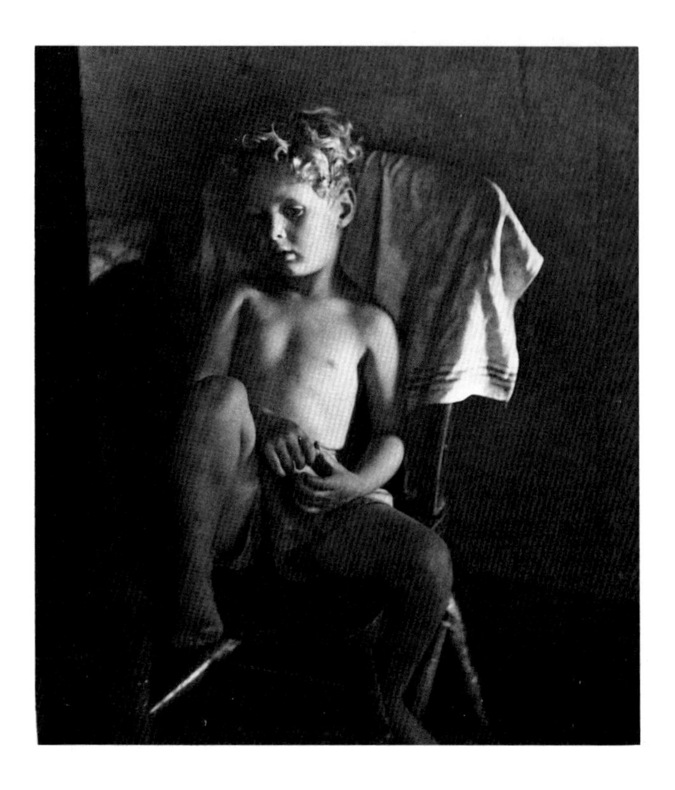

That afternoon is spent discussing a troubling question: Should Dylan go again to America? He himself seems ambivalent, but Caitlin is dead-set against another trip. As John struggles to be objective, I remain detached, not wishing to be caught up in matters which are complicated, emotionally charged and not my responsibility. No definite decision will be made before we leave Laugharne, but it soon becomes clear that Dylan, shifting ground, has decided to go. John addresses practical matters: bookings, the possible advantage of Dylan's working in California on an opera with Stravinsky, the chance of repeating the successful reading performances of *Under Milk Wood*. Caitlin says she does not want to be left alone in Laugharne with Colm while Dylan again gives himself over to the care of any one of the many women he has met in New York, with some of whom she knows he is still in correspondence. She writes of them later: "These thieves of my love, which I was so presumptuously sure was mine only, I bitterly, jealously resented, with all the primitive catfish instincts that I didn't even know were there..."

"I have longed to move
away but am afraid;
Some life, yet unspent,
might explode
Out of the old lie burning
on the ground,
And, crackling into the
air, leave me half-blind."

Soon after the unresolved discussion on the balcony of the Boathouse, I take a series of family pictures in Mrs. Thomas's garden. Everyone sits upon, or gathers around, an old park bench; the children squirming, making faces or balking at the occasion, Mrs. Thomas gently keeping them in order, Caitlin looking happy, and Dylan being the patient papa. His reaction is solemn, even benign. If he is bored, no one can tell.

(Dylan was always a cooperative subject. Sometimes he had a tendency to clown—after all, his reputation as a ham had to be kept up. On the whole, I think he enjoyed having his picture taken. Never was he recalcitrant about accepting an occasional direction of mine, or resentful of the time photographic sessions sometimes took. Whether his attitude was out of deference to me or came from an unconscious wish to be "immortalized in a moment," I have never known. Perhaps he just became used to my presence.)

That evening at the Boathouse, we have what I like to remember as the "disastrous duck." Someone has given Caitlin a wild duck with the admonition that to overcook it is tantamount to serious crime. The result of her caution is that the duck, which John imprudently agrees to carve, is so tough that it resists penetration of knife or fork. It bounces onto the floor; and re-attacked, it spurts blood like a miniature geyser. With appetites diminished, we make our meal of homemade bread, vegetables and milk.

When it is time to leave, Caitlin insists that both John and Dylan accompany me along Cliff Walk to the Pelican. A woman has been knifed to death not long before, and the suspect, still at large, is a deaf-mute who formerly lived nearby. A silly precaution?—yet we do as Caitlin has asked. More scared than we will admit, we giggle and laugh unseemingly at Dylan's ghost stories and realize, on reaching the village, we've been holding hands the entire way!

"Ghosts whooed like owls in the long nights when I dared not look over my shoulder . . ."

On a Sunday afternoon, John and I take Dylan and his mother in our little rented car to tour the other side of the river Taf, a peninsula whose villages have names like Llanybri, Llanstephan, Llangynog, Llangain, Llanllwch. (It is easy to understand why Dylan, tongue in cheek, chose "Llareggub" as the town's name in *Under Milk Wood.)*

The network of narrow roads is mostly unmarked, but Mrs. Thomas seems to know her way as if by divination, and we soon find Fern Hill, the farm which had belonged to her sister, Annie Jones. Yellow-washed house and white barns stand close to each other and the green fields come right up to them. The current owner invites John, Dylan and me to go through the house at our leisure while he chats outside with Mrs. Thomas. The interior is dark, illuminated occasionally by pointed shafts of light shining through Gothic-like windows. This definitely is not the "lilting" and "gay" house of Dylan's childhood: gone are the stuffed fox, the case of china and pewter, the brass candlesticks, the ". . .tinted photograph of Annie . . . with high hair and her breasts coming out." Even the dust on the carpet is gone! Clean as a sea-washed bone, and as lifeless, the parlor is tidily filled with overstuffed furniture, large table lamps and forgotten aspidistra. The sight depresses Dylan, so we go outside, pick over the fallen apples, walk a bit in the "fields of praise," and, after joining the owner and thanking him for his hospitality, continue on our expedition to the Chapel Newydd, the burial place of Annie Jones and her husband, Jim. When we arrive, Mrs. Thomas is near tears. Dylan's feelings are unfathomable and, loath to photograph them at the graveside, I take a few discreet shots of them walking toward it. The dreary gray stone, and the gravel fill of the grave itself, are relieved somewhat by the bright gold lettering of the names, and by a squat bell jar covering an arrangement of artificial leaves and flowers.

"I stand, for this memorial's
sake, alone
In the snivelling hours
with dead, humped Ann
Whose hooded, fountain
heart once fell in
puddles
Round the parched
worlds of Wales and
drowned each sun . . ."

ER COF ANNWYL AM
Annie Jones
MOUNT PLEASANT LLANGAIN
HUNODD CHWEF 7, 1933, YN 70 OED.
HEFYD EI PHRIOD
James Jones
HUNODD MEDI 3, 1942, YN 78 OED.
HENFFYCH DDYDD CAWN ETO GYFRODD

*". . . it was lovely, the hay
Fields high as the
house . . ."*

The "snail-horned" church at Llanybri and its graveyard are our next destination. From there we can look back and identify the Boathouse, the old Ferry House to one side of it, Dylan's writing shack to the left, and Laugharne Castle down the estuary at the bottom of the village.

Then we set off to find farming relatives of Mrs. Thomas. After a false start or two, we come to a dirt wagon-path leading to a large cluster of off-white structures. Hordes of people and animals pour out to greet us, all living cozily together in what appears to be one vast abode. But closer inspection shows outbuildings for cows, chickens, pigs and sheep. Mrs. Thomas and Dylan are taken up by cousins young and old. As at Fern Hill, the utterly simple interior of the house is too dark to photograph with the limited equipment I have brought, so I go outside with one of the cousins assigned to feed the animals. After taking several shots of the orderly countryside, haystacks and sheep, I join the others, only to find myself bewildered by their Welsh or Anglo-Welsh conversation. The central room is bursting with relatives, while in a little anteroom sits their ranking matriarch, a woman nearly a hundred years old, dressed in shiny black taffeta.

We leave, in order not to drive after dark, and shortly come upon a brother of Mrs. Thomas, whom she calls "old Tom." Widowed for forty years, he speaks hardly a word. His most distinguished feature is a tall, rounded felt hat, which, I am told, is his constant companion. Once a year Mrs. Thomas goes to tidy his house.

We proceed to Llanstephan, which, like Laugharne, is on a wide estuary. Its houses, too, are simple, small white, yellow and pink; and a castle much grander, though in no better repair than the one in Laugharne, commands the skyline. Here and nearby, Dylan had spent some of the summer days of his childhood with relatives.

It has been a long trip, but Dylan seems peaceful and not interested in drinking. We are all in a happy mood, and the gloom of the discussion about Dylan's and Caitlin's plans is dispersed for a time, though not forgotten. John and I set off for London the following day.

"Beyond that unknown Wales with its wild names like peals of bells in the darkness . . ."

"Immortalized in a moment . . ."

To go back to my first meeting with Dylan and Caitlin is to go back to a cold January evening in 1952, at my home in Millbrook, New York, where they arrived with John from New York. Caitlin I could hardly see, so swathed was she in a fur hat, coat and boots. I couldn't see Dylan either for the bulk of the brown parka he was wearing. Quickly divested of these encumbrances, they warmed themselves before the fire.

Caitlin was a startlingly beautiful woman with ringlets of blond hair, a clear, highly colored complexion, regular features and a full but trim figure. Dylan was short, wiry-haired, pudgy-faced and chubby.

In her book *Leftover Life to Kill,* Caitlin described their appearances: ". . . in our first, know-nothing lamb-sappy days . . . Dylan may have been a skinny, springy lambkin, but I was more like its buxom mother then, and distinctly recollect carrying him across streams under one arm; 'till the roles were reversed, and he blew out, and I caved in, through the pressure of family life, and the advent of holy-fire destroying babies."

Everyone was weary on this night of their arrival, and after supper we retired early.

Next morning, the fields a dazzling white, the sky blue and clear, the sun bright and the wind sharp, Dylan, John and I started outside for a short walk and picture-taking. I had been making a series of portraits of poets for the Poetry Center at the YM-YWHA in New York, and Dylan was on my list. As we went out the front door, Dylan spotted a large bare wisteria vine and immediately entwined himself in it, laughing, smiling, smirking, then sinking as if crucified. I was enchanted by his pleasure in being before the camera. Needing to hurry because of the cold, I used up several rolls of film on Dylan by the wisteria, then in front of stone walls, in haystacks and with John, sitting around a disused silo.

"I who was rich was made
the richer
By sipping at the vine of
days."

Meanwhile, Caitlin had gone to her room, ostensibly to keep up her journal—Dylan and she having been commissioned to do a book about their trip to the United States. She did come down long enough for me to photograph them in my bare "studio," the top room of a small garage inadequately warmed by a pot-bellied stove. There Caitlin came to life, posing with Dylan as a loving wife, enjoying herself despite the chilly air.

Dylan, eager for Caitlin to see something of "typical America," was delighted when John suggested taking them out to lunch and showing them some neighboring sights. I stayed home and heard about the trip on their return: Howard Johnson's—hot dogs, hamburgers and ice cream; Vassar College—lank-haired girls, dirty sneakers, blue jeans and sweatshirts. Caitlin's comment that "they look like intellectual witches" I could hardly fault, for I had been a student in the days of clean hair, polished shoes, skirts, sweaters and pearls. Their next stop was a tavern in Rhinebeck complete with horse brasses, juke box, pinball machine and beer.

That evening my other guests appeared—a couple, both professors, and mutual friends of John's and mine. An hour or more after they had arrived, Caitlin was still sequestered in her room. Finally, when dinner was already overdone, she came downstairs, greeted our guests perfunctorily, then sat silent and detached in a far corner and began to draw cartoons of Dylan on the back of a "Between the Acts" cigar box. Still concentrating silently, she proceeded to draw John and one guest on the cover of a box of cheese.

Once at table, however, Caitlin dominated the conversation. She kept interrupting or correcting Dylan, and made us all so uncomfortable that we were relieved when, back in the living room, she again sought out her corner and continued to draw, or to leaf through magazines. An endless evening.

That night in bed I thought about Caitlin's behavior. She had not been impolite to me directly, but her remoteness and rudeness were puzzling. She was very attractive, and she was also strong-willed; she had no need for such defenses. My sleepy conclusion was that she was defensive because she did not know any of us except John and she had never been to America before. Perhaps she resented taking a back seat to her husband. I liked her despite my discomfort with her, and hoped to be able to reassure her if the opportunity arose.

The next morning John went to Boston. I drove Dylan and Caitlin to New York and left them at the Hotel Earle in Greenwich Village. Throughout their stay with me Dylan had drunk very little. He was amusing, gentle with Caitlin and polite to everyone.

I photographed him several times in New York, but I would not see Caitlin again until that summer day in Laugharne when she waved to me from the muddy banks of the river Taf.

Dylan's lecture and reading schedule after he left Millbrook lasted four grueling months in a coast-to-coast marathon which left him shattered. His tensions increased with each performance. Over-drinking, partying too much, he tried to meet the demands of well-meaning but misdirected hosts by gulping his food (when he wasn't retching), tossing back double whiskeys, and somehow stumbling, often on time, onto still another stage where he usually performed brilliantly.

But despite his pleasure in the adulation he received, he felt trapped. Writing to a friend for money, he said: "There are so many petty jobs which . . . stop me writing as I could wish to write. . . . It is so difficult for me to live and to keep my family alive."

"Now I am a man no more
no more
And a black reward for a
roaring life."

He read at the Poetry Center three times on this trip, always to a packed house. Standing barely five feet five and a half inches in his blue canvas gum-soled shoes, a dark blue suit shiny from too many pressings, and sporting a blue-and-white dotted bow tie, with his voice projecting forcefully, melodically, he appeared much taller. He dominated his audience without any apparent difficulty . . . but difficulty he had. After a reading, exhausted, he hovered between exhilaration and collapse. The pendulum usually swung towards the nearest bar.

That fall, when he returned to Laugharne and to Caitlin almost penniless, he wrote to the Princess Caetani, editor of *Botteghe Oscure,* apologizing for not having sent her all of "Llareggub": "I . . . flew over America like a damp, ranting bird; boomed and fiddled while home was burning; carried with me all the time, my unfinished letters, my dying explanations and self-accusations, my lonely half of a looney maybe-play, in a heavy, hurtful bunch . . . I made money, and it went, and I returned with none . . ."

On his third trip, which began in April of 1953 and lasted about six weeks, he remained in the eastern United States to give some fifteen readings, but mostly to perfect and perform his "looney maybe-play," whose name now was *Under Milk Wood.* With the help of Liz Reitell, John's assistant at the Poetry Center, Dylan began to train the actors, some of whom she had selected from the Y's clerical pool—Dion Allen, Allen Collins, Roy Poole, Sada Thompson and Nancy Wickwire.

"I . . . flew over America like a damp, ranting bird . . ."

Five performers and Dylan, taking fifty-four parts, made up the entire cast. There were to be no scenes, no sets, no acting except for voices and gestures. The actors sat on high stools against a plain dark background, their scripts on lecterns in front of them.

At the Manhattan apartment of one of the actors they began to work. First familiarizing them with the script and then running through it many times, Dylan coached them relentlessly in pronunciation and sentence rhythm. Unlike his father and mother, Dylan spoke no Welsh; but he knew Anglo-Welsh intimately and insisted his actors use it accurately.

He chain-smoked but drank lightly during these informal rehearsals. The actors had his complete attention and responded quickly and sensitively to his instructions. Liz sat aside, followed the script and made occasional suggestions. Soon it was time to move rehearsals to the Kaufmann Auditorium at the "Y."

On a day of one of the last rehearsals before the first performance, I met Dylan and Liz in an Irish bar near the Poetry Center. Dylan looked wan and worse than I had ever seen him. His speech was thick and he alternated between wild gestures and a tearful blubbering. He said that he could not rehearse—not possibly. He could not even get to the Y. Desperate because we knew he wanted so much to make his cherished play a success in America, we cajoled and pleaded with him—but to no avail. We were at our wits' end as to how to help him and had given up when he gathered his wobbly round body together and said he thought he could make it. Relieved, we made our way uncertainly down the street and arrived safely. He vomited and passed out on the couch in the Green Room.

"Love the words," he told them. "Love *the words."*

Meanwhile, the actors had come in. Liz shook Dylan awake; he muttered that he absolutely could not work. Yet, somehow, from some deep core of his being, he found strength to get up and put his cast through their most electrifying experience to date. I could not believe, as I photographed, hearing him admonish them to "love the words . . . . *Love* the words," that he was the same man I had seen a few minutes before: a disoriented hulk had become a driving, inspiring teacher. This almost miraculous power of recuperation Caitlin had observed in him many times: "One moment he was flat out, in utter self-abandonment; coughing and heaving up his heart, down to the soles of his boots; the next, dolled up, like a puppy's supper, dapper and spruce, or as near as he could get to it."

May fourteenth, day of the premiere performance of *Under Milk Wood* at Kaufmann Auditorium, Dylan, Liz and two typists came to my apartment on 88th Street, just a few blocks from the Y. Dylan had not yet finished the conclusion of the play and he wanted to make some revisions of other sections of it. As fast as he could write, the typists punched out various parts and someone took them to the Y so that the actors could rehearse them. But there was still no satisfactory ending. Dylan just could not resolve the play. When John arrived and had had a chance to confer with Liz, they concluded that for Dylan's sake and that of everyone else, the performance had best be called off. That prospect galvanized Dylan into a gigantic effort and, less than an hour before curtain time, he improvised an ending that would do temporarily.

*"To begin at the beginning . . .
At the sea end of town, Mr and Mrs Floyd, the cocklers, are sleeping as quiet as death, side by wrinkled side, toothless, salt and brown, like two old kippers in a box."*

*"But I always think as we tumble into bed
Of little Willy Wee who is dead, dead, dead."*

"I saw you talking to a saint this morning. Saint Polly Garter. She was martyred again last night. Mrs Organ Morgan saw her with Mr Waldo."

"Down in the dusking town, Mae Rose Cottage, still lying in clover, listens to the nannygoats chew, draws circles of lipstick round her nipples."

After Dylan had written the last word, I glanced at him and realized he could not go on stage looking as he did—his pale face seemed to have grown an extra length of beard and he was sweating copiously. We went into my bathroom, he washed up, and after I had applied makeup and suntan powder to his face, we walked the short distance to the Poetry Center. There was less than half an hour to go before curtain. The actors were frantically reading over the last few sentences.

When the house lights dimmed and then slowly came up as each actor spoke, the audience, not knowing at all what to expect, was quiet for the first several minutes. At last a few people tittered and then, realizing that this was not an erudite work beyond their comprehension but an affectionately bawdy sketch of a village, everyone joined in the laughter that kept bursting forth until the curtain fell. Fifteen curtain calls later, Dylan came out alone. Only those in the first few rows could see the tears on his cheeks.

"Here's your arsenic, dear.
And your weedkiller biscuit.
I've throttled your parakeet.
I've spat in the vases.
I've put cheese in the mouseholes.
Here's your . . .
(Door creaks open)
. . . nice tea, dear."

"I'm fast. *I'm a bad lot. God will strike me dead. I'm seventeen. I'll go to hell."*

"I am a draper mad with love. I love you more than all the flannelette and calico, candlewick, dimity, crash and merino, tussore, cretonne, crépon, muslin, poplin, ticking and twill in the whole Cloth Hall of the world . . ."

UNDER MILK WOOD

With the Original New York Cast

FEATURING DYLAN THOMAS

Actor	Roles
ROY POOLE	Captain Cat Jack Black Mr. Waldo Organ Morgan Ocky Milkman Mr. Pugh Voice of a Guide Book Billy
NANCY WICKWIRE	Rosie Probert Mrs. Beynon Gossamer Beynon Mrs. Utah Watkins Mrs. Cherry Owen Mrs. Willy Nilly Mrs. Pugh Mrs. Dai Bread Two Polly Garter Bessie Bighead First Neighbor 2nd Woman
DION ALLEN	2nd Voice 4th Drowned Mr. Pritchard Cherry Owen Willy Nilly Lord Cut-Glass Johnny Cristo
DYLAN THOMAS	1st Voice 2nd Drowned 5th Drowned Reverend Eli Jenkins
SADA THOMPSON	Myfanwy Price Mrs. Ogmore-Pritchard Mrs. Organ Morgan Lily Smalls Mae Rose Cottage Mary Ann Sailors Gwennie 2nd Neighbor 1st Woman Child's Voice Mrs. Dai Bread One
ALLEN F. COLLINS	1st Drowned 3rd Drowned Mog Edwards Thomas the Death Mr. Ogmore Butcher Beynon Utah Watkins P. C. Attilla Rees Sinbad Sailors Dai Bread Nogood Boyo Dicky

Soon after John and I had left Laugharne that September of 1953, word followed that Dylan would come to New York without Caitlin. Warned by physicians both in America and in London to stop drinking if he was to survive, he arrived on October nineteenth, several days late. This was his fourth and last trip.

Staying as usual at the Chelsea Hotel, Dylan had become by now more deeply involved with Liz, more dependent upon her affection and her competence in matters he found impossible to deal with.

Under Milk Wood, with its original cast and a revised and final ending, was performed again at the Poetry Center October twenty-fourth. Afterwards, I gave a party for the actors. Dylan was subdued, refused drinks and kept saying that he had "seen the gates of hell." He looked like it. Keeping up by telephone, I knew that he was ill in body and spirit. John's book, *Dylan Thomas in America,* records the ominous moods and events of those last days, but he would not learn for twenty-five years that Dylan had arrived in America with his health already severely impaired. Visiting Philip Burton at his home in Key West, John wrote in his journal for 1978:

> I learned of Dylan's last day in London and of an episode which, had he not kept it to himself, might have allowed Lizzie and other friends in New York to help him before he was beyond help.
>
> Burton, a program director for the BBC (he produced Dylan's "Return Journey"), had invited him to his flat for a leavetaking drink on the afternoon of October 13th when, according to Burton, Dylan was in an uncommonly unhappy and meditative mood. As they chatted—over a single drink, Burton recalls—Dylan said that he felt his lyric writing days were over, that from then on he would have to concentrate on his "own brand" of writing for the stage and radio. When Dylan asked if he might take "a bit of a lie-down," Burton showed him to a bedroom, drew the blinds and, at Dylan's request, set an alarm clock to ring within the hour.

Settled down with a book, Burton heard the alarm go off and waited for Dylan's reappearance. When there was no further sound for half an hour, Burton entered the bedroom and found Dylan where he'd left him, now breathing heavily. Calling his name and getting no response, he tried with a shake to bring him to, without success. He was about to phone for a doctor when Dylan sat up and rubbed his eyes.

"How long did *that* one last?" asked Dylan.

"*That* one . . .?"

"The blackout . . . it's the second one today. Poor Louis MacNeice took me to lunch and thought he had a corpse on his hands."

On November fifth, John called from St. Vincent's Hospital in New York—Dylan was in a coma. John, Liz and a few friends were there and word of what had happened was soon widespread. The hospital's waiting room began to fill with more friends and hangers-on. Caitlin, in Wales, was informed immediately. But with no family or official representative on the spot, the awesome burden of decisions fell on John and Liz, while closest friends did what they could to help.

Dylan lay under an oxygen tent, his eyes open but unfocused, his breathing heavy, his face blotchy. The term used to us to describe his condition was "a severe insult to the brain," due to direct alcoholic poisoning of the brain cells. Indeed, Dylan had said to Liz before he collapsed: "I've had eighteen straight whiskies. I think that's the record."

The number probably was a Dylanesque exaggeration but the effect was catastrophic.

The physicians at St. Vincent's, at first not certain what had been given to him by the doctor called to the hotel where he collapsed before being admitted, were not in a position to do much for him beyond basic emergency care. However, the longer he remained unconscious, the less chance he had of normal recovery. Specialists were called in, but it was too late for effective heroic measures.

On the night of November eighth Caitlin arrived. Driven to the brink of madness by the sight of Dylan so totally unreachable, she lost all control. She smoked in his room, snatched a crucifix from the wall and broke it, assaulted John and an attendant nun and bit an orderly. Looking on helplessly at the damage she was doing to others and to herself, I suggested that a physician be called. The appalled officials at St. Vincent's wished to send her to Bellevue, Manhattan's principal psychiatric care center, but none of us wanted her admitted there. Finally, the doctor who had cared for Dylan made arrangements for her to go to a private hospital in Astoria, Long Island. Drained by her experiences, which included a short period of strait-jacket restraint, she went meekly into the ambulance with her friends, Rose and David Slivka. What startled me more than her docility was her appearance. She still looked, as Dylan had said of her, like "the princess on top of a Christmas tree!"

Around one o'clock on the afternoon of the ninth, Dylan, who had not regained consciousness, slipped away, unable even to rage against his own darkness.

Home that night, spent, dazed, I emptied my pockets while preparing for bed. A small piece of paper fell to the floor. On it his last nurse had written me a receipt—a sad memento:

11·9·53
Dylan Thomas
From 11·9·53 to 11·9·53
One 8 hrs. $14.50
Rec'd. Margaret McIntyre

In the care of Rose and David, Caitlin was released from the hospital in Astoria immediately after Dylan died, and I joined her at their Greenwich Village house. Heartbroken, yet able to cope with the reality of her loss, she wrote out cables for me to send to her children and to Dylan's mother. When Caitlin asked me to go with her to the funeral parlor, I went for her sake, but could not face Dylan's open casket. She dutifully appeared at the memorial service for Dylan at St. Luke's Episcopal Chapel of Trinity Parish, where, as I had promised, I rescued her from the inevitable crowd whose condolences she would have found a torture.

When the SS *United States* sailed for England, Caitlin accompanied Dylan's body back to Laugharne. The trip was a nightmare. She feigned a fit in order to get away from an incompatible cabin-mate. One day she wandered into the hold of the ship to find some of the crew noisily eating their lunches while sitting on top of her husband's casket.

In Laugharne at last and reunited with her children, Caitlin undertook her last public ordeal, to bury Dylan on November twenty-fourth in St. Martin's churchyard. Friends who attended wrote that it was a beautiful day and a very moving occasion. Most of his nearest friends were there. They were all worried about Caitlin; but she went through the ceremony surprisingly well. It was her future that concerned everyone.

A simple white wooden cross marked the grave and has remained unchanged, except for fancier lettering, for twenty-eight years.

"At poor peace I sing
To you strangers . . ."

"I, born of flesh and ghost, was neither
A ghost nor man, but mortal ghost.
And I was struck down by death's feather."

A few weeks after Dylan's funeral I received a long letter from Caitlin, written at the Boathouse. She thanked me warmly and extravagantly for support that I had given her and asked me to help her clear up "a few gnawing bafflements," such as, "What was the acute thing that the doctors said happened to Dylan a day or so before he collapsed? And how much had Elizabeth Reitell to do with it all?" She begged me to tell the truth, however it might hurt her. John, she felt, had not been fair with her: ". . . too much hedging." He treated her, she claimed, "like a maniacal marauding animal, which is true up to a point, but not entirely. Unfortunately there is the seeing eye left. He wrote me a very sweet letter, but he is too sweet altogether. I should prefer a little verminous pepper . . . the trouble is, I love, respect and believe John, but want to kill him."

And then a postscript:

> I can't tell you what hell it is being back here, with Dylan so close, in that stinking rotten churchyard—It is beyond saying—Forget it. Please write to me, *please*. Thank you for the beautiful photographs. I wish I was dead. I tried and failed.

I responded as best I could, telling her that the "acute thing" probably referred to Dylan's boast that he had had a record eighteen straight whiskies. As for Liz, I admired her, though we were not close friends. Painful as it might be for Caitlin to hear, Liz was genuinely attached to Dylan and I knew that she had discouraged his drinking. Under the circumstances, it was fortunate for Dylan that she stood by him.

My concluding words, which I feared sounded "preachy," urged her, for her children's sake as well as her own, to try to think constructively about a new life, and not to lose touch with me.

"Years and years and years ago, when I was a boy, when there were wolves in Wales, and birds the color of red-flannel petticoats whisked past the harp-shaped hills . . ."

Dylan had been dead four years when I went to Swansea, his birthplace, under the guidance of Vernon Watkins, his close friend and long-time literary correspondent. Vernon lived in a small house in Pennard, south of Swansea on the Gower Peninsula, with his wife, Gwen, and their two children. A spare, spry man with thick, prematurely white hair and deepset, penetrating, but kindly eyes, he worked in a bank in Swansea, but his real vocation was poetry. A charming and enthusiastic guide, he took me one day to number five Cwmdonkin Drive, where Dylan was born and raised, and to Cwmdonkin Park, a step across the street, and his favorite play area as a boy.

> . . . And the park itself was a world within the world of the sea-town. Quite near where I lived, so near that on summer evenings I could listen in my bed to the voices of older children playing ball on the sloping paper-littered bank, the park was full of terrors and treasures. . . .

At night he hung around the railway lines, walked the downtown streets with his pals near "ghostly Ebenezer Chapel," picking up girls, or, with special friends, compared notes on poctry.

The view from the top of Cwmdonkin Drive, as well as that from Dylan's bedroom, looked over shiny tile roofs of nearly identical terrace houses, then down to the curving shore with its big tides creating pattern upon pattern. To the right lay the Mumbles, small islands lined up as if marching to sea and infinity. Number five Cwmdonkin Drive was, like its neighbors, wood-trimmed and constructed of grey stucco and plain slate. Its only concession to decoration was three rows of fish-scale slate in the pediments of the two gables on the street side.

The owner welcomed us inside. We peered about, mostly out of windows, since the interior looked and felt unlived-in. A wooden lamp had "Twenty-Four Years," a poem Dylan had written for his birthday, in calligraphy on one side of its parchment shade. This tribute illuminated a corner of the living room. Vernon, whispering that the house was nothing like what it had been when Dylan's parents lived here, suggested we leave. Thanking the owner, we did.

Across the street in Cwmdonkin Park, the once-open reservoir where Dylan and his truant chums had sailed boats and harassed swans was now covered over. But everything else remained unchanged: the rustically decorated Victorian bandstand where he had fist fights and listened to the brass band; the chained cups from which "the hunchback in the park" had drunk; the uncultivated "jungles," as well as manicured green slopes and a play area. It was late afternoon. I recalled the end of a story Dylan wrote about a visit to the park after World War II:

NARRATOR

We had reached the last gate. Dusk drew around us and the town. I said: What has become of him now?

PARK-KEEPER

Dead.

NARRATOR

The Park-keeper said . . .

[The park bell rings.]

PARK-KEEPER

Dead . . . Dead . . . Dead . . . Dead . . . Dead . . . Dead.

"... the park was full of terrors and treasures."

"I was born in a large Welsh town at the beginning of the Great War — an ugly, lovely town (or so it was and is to me), crawling, sprawling by a long and splendid curving shore where truant boys and sandfield boys and old men from nowhere, beachcombed, idled and paddled, watched the dock-bound ships or the ships steaming away into wonder and India, magic and China . . ."

On the way back to Pennard, Vernon pointed out some of Dylan's old pubs, among them the Mermaid at the Mumbles. In the early years of their marriage, he told me, Dylan and Caitlin would often go to a pub for an evening's beer or two; but if they found the atmosphere dull, they livened up the place by staging a quarrel. As their voices became louder, their language and accusations more outrageous, other drinkers joined in and a free-for-all followed.

At home after such an evening, Dylan's and Caitlin's passionate attachment would rekindle. Over the years, said Vernon, they found this game more and more destructive. Making up became less easy, and once uttered, insults were not as quickly forgiven.

The next day we drove and walked all over the wild Gower Peninsula. At first we seemed to have it all to ourselves. But soon, nearby and far, we noticed other people; boys, boys and girls, families, solitary men and women; some carrying fresh-caught fish, feathers, rocks, sea-whitened sticks and other prizes.

Vernon, agile as a boy, ran up and down the cliffs while I panted behind him, begging him to slow down so that I could photograph him as a man, not as a mountain goat! We went on to look at the Worm's Head, an enormous rock jutting into the sea. Its long, low-lying neck would be submerged completely at high tide. To me it looked less like a garden worm than like a sea-going behemoth that, venturing too close, was trapped by its tail to the mainland.

After a sandwich and a rest in the grotto we all climbed up the precipice to Rhossilli—no more than a cluster of houses and a meagerly stocked general store. It was what lay below that was exciting: the vast sweep of Carmarthen Bay and white-capped waves rolling in to form a beach half a mile wide and at least five miles long. On shore at the foot of a dark hill was an enormous white mansion-like building and miniscule sticks and white dots, which, I suddenly realized, were people and sheep.

Dylan wrote about this wild terrain and Rhossilli Beach in another tale of his boyhood. "Extraordinary Little Cough" (his real name was George Hooping) is referred to either as "Cough" or by the full title, which also is the name of the story. The inept member of the group of boys who go camping near Rhossilli Beach, Cough is the constant object of their teasing:

> "He can't swim."
> "He can't run."
> "He can't learn."
> "He can't bowl."
> "He can't bat."
> "And I bet he can't make water."

Cough, however, meets their challenge, and, he hopes, the admiration of the girls they have picked up:

> . . . We were old and alone, sitting beyond desire in the middle of the night, when George appeared, like a ghost, in the firelight and stood there, trembling, until I said: "Where've you been? You've been gone hours. Why are you trembling like that?". . .
> George Hooping could hardly stand. I put my hand on his shoulder to steady him, but he pushed it away.
> "I've been running on Rhossilli sands! I ran every bit of it! You said I couldn't, and I did! I've been running and running!"

"I've been running on Rhossilli sands! I ran every bit of it! You said I couldn't and I did. I've been running and running!"

"The dream has sucked the
sleeper of his faith
That shrouded men might
marrow as they fly."

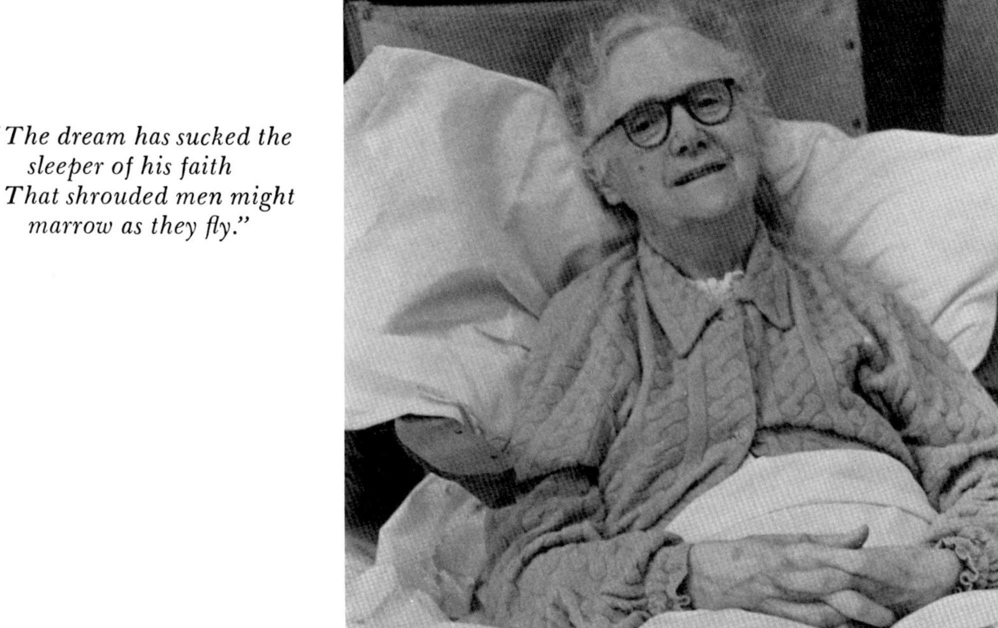

When I leave the Gower and Swansea, I feel I have understood Dylan the boy better than Dylan the man.

From there I journey to Port Talbot, where Mrs. Thomas, bedridden, is being cared for by friends. Then I join Caitlin once more in Laugharne, where she is staying at the Boathouse with all of the children.

Feeling stupid, I utter the banal, foolish things older people say to children they haven't seen for years. Llewelyn is a tall attractive youth of eighteen, Aeron now has the figure of a young woman, and Colm, no longer a cherub, is a lean and impish school boy.

Caitlin and I have a chastening and affectionate visit, wading in the mud of the estuary, sunning on the balcony and visiting Ivy and Ebie at Browns. The bar has been redecorated with a wild, patterned wallpaper. When we all gather at Dylan's and Caitlin's accustomed table, Caitlin sits beneath a photograph taken in their early married days. The picture has hung there for years. Who took it, no one seems to know.

That evening alone, we talk of Dylan and the miserable days in New York, of Liz, about mutual friends and about her own uncertain future. She asks me how John is.

When it's time to part she says, "Tell the bastard I love him anyway." Fighting tears as I turn from the Boathouse door, I hear her say, "Don't ever forget me."

"Dylan and dying, Dylan and dying, they don't go together; or is it that they were bound to go together; he said so often enough, but I did not heed him."

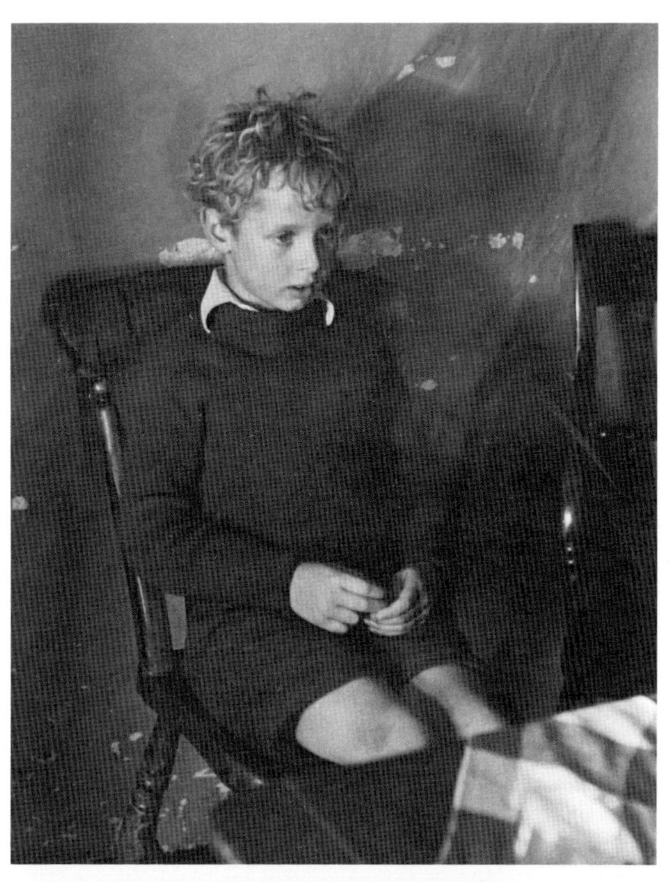

"And all the people of the lulled and dumbfound town are sleeping now."

Oh as I was young and easy in the mercy of his means
time held me green and dying
though I sang in my chains like the sea
DYLAN

Postscript

Dylan's mother died in July 1958 in Port Talbot, Wales. She had been cared for during her last years by dear friends, Hetty Owen and her husband Ken.

Caitlin lives in Rome south of Trastevere in a spacious, airy apartment across the Tiber from S. Paolo fuori le Mura. With her is her longtime Sicilian friend Giuseppe Fazio and their son Francesco, who is now 18. When I lunched with them there in the spring of 1980, I found a happy welcome and a still handsome Caitlin.

Aeron (Aeronwy) Thomas Ellis, 39, lives with her husband Trefor and their two young children in Surrey, not far from London. Huw Dylan is 6 years old and looks like his grandfather. Hannah Florence, 3, is named for her great-grandmother. Aeron, bilingual, goes twice a year to Italy to teach contemporary English literature to teenagers. She also tours, reading her father's and her own poetry; has published two slim volumes; and reads, on tape, stories for children.

After long and accomplished work in advertising with J. Walter Thompson in Australia, Llewelyn, 42, lives in London with his daughter, Jennie. He is writing science fiction.

His younger brother, Colm, 32, lives with his wife in Australia. Since his graduation with top honors from Canberra University, he has had a varied career, including driving a taxi and working for Customs and Excise.

Laugharne, which I revisited in July 1981, has changed, but not radically. There is a disposal plant at the foot of Sir John's hill, making it considerably less photogenic. A small ceramics factory near the town hall turns out rough wares, including mugs depicting the Boathouse on one side and Dylan's profile on the other. Cliff Walk is called Dylan's Walk, but its sign was not in evidence when I was there. Caitlin sold the Boathouse years ago. It remained under various sponsors, not as it was, but nevertheless intact and open to the public. Photographs of mine and others, and silkscreened adaptations of these photographs, were scattered about. Paint was peeling. Some rooms had no furniture. The balcony was in poor repair. The interior of the work-shack showed no signs that it was ever Dylan's. The exterior in early July 1980 was painted a garish blue, and had on its façade, if you can call it a façade, a crude mural of dubious iconography.

All this is changing, for house, garden and writing shack have been taken over by the Carmarthen District Council, which has hired the South Wales Tourism Council to deal with day-to-day operation. The Boathouse and shack will be refurbished, and will remain as a memorial in the form of a museum.

The Castle, bare of ivy, was being restored by the Ministry of the Environment. Its walls were not available to be scaled for views to seaward.

Browns Hotel is no longer a public place. Both Ivy and Ebie Williams are dead, and I was told on reliable authority that Billy Williams fell "afoul of the law." I like to think that the three of them and Dylan are playing "nap" somewhere.

In the new cemetery, where Dylan is buried, many more graves surround him. His white wooden cross remains as it was, but with new black lettering.

Despite these changes, Laugharne remains a charming village by the sea, whose main attraction—apart from its site—is its evocation of Dylan. Fern Hill is protected by a high, barred iron gate, where a big sign reads "Guard Dogs in Action." One unkempt Afghan and two small terriers, scratching and wagging their tails, were busily doing their duty.

Swansea has grown somewhat, suffering what most cities suffer in the name of progress—more buildings, more people, less open space—but Cwmdonkin Drive and Dylan's house at Number 5 seemed unchanged. In Cwmdonkin Park, the chained cups are missing from the fountain where the hunchback drank, and the bandstand is no more, but the park does boast two memorials to Dylan—one, a triangular shelter of bricks and wood-beamed roof donated by the Oakleigh House School and Swansea City Council (1975), has carved on its graffiti-invaded wooden interior: "This sea-town was my world. And the park itself was a world within the world of the sea-town."

The more handsome and as yet unvandalized memorial is an irregularly shaped stone at the water's edge of a small pond. Incised on it are the last three lines from "Fern Hill": "Oh as I was young and easy in the mercy of his means/Time held me green and dying/Though I sang in my chains like the sea."

The Gower has remained wild. Perhaps many of the young prefer hang-gliding to hiking and fishing. Certainly there were more campers—called caravans by the British, but the cliffs and springing grass and the golden sands of Rhossilli are, we must hope, there forever.

On St. David's Day, March 1, 1982, a memorial plaque to Dylan, made of Welsh stone, was unveiled in the Poets' Corner, South Transept of Westminster Abbey. On it are inscribed the last two lines of "Fern Hill."

Technical Notes

All photographs (except five taken in 1981) were made with a range finder camera, the Leica III F: 50mm, 35mm, and 80mm Nikon lenses were adapted. A Kilfitt Kilar 150mm f/3.5 lens attachment on a Pentax body took care of long shots, and a twin lens Rolleiflex 3.5 F with a 75mm Tessar lens was invaluable. Two Weston Master V light meters—one for a back-up—determined exposures.

Super XX, emulsion speed 100, a beautiful black-and-white film, was my stand-by. It is available now in long-roll quantities for bulk loading. Color film was Kodachrome, emulsion speed 10, and Ektachrome with a speed of 25.

All pictures were taken with available light. Because of weight and bulk restrictions, I traveled with neither flash nor tripod, but carried a chain which I used occasionally as a monopod.

Recent photographs were made with a single lens reflex camera, the Olympus OM-1 equipped with a 50mm, a 24mm, and a 75-150 zoom lens. A Rollei 35 with f/3.5, 40mm Tessar lens completed my camera inventory.

Black-and-white film used was Plus X, ASA 125 or Tri X, ASA 400. Color was Kodachrome 64.

Author's Acknowledgments

It is said often that writing is a lonely occupation. I am not so sure!

Judith Bachmann, my assistant, has lasting gratitude for her support and constant good humor when it was needed most. Her skills, too, made working an edifying delight.

Louise Pittaway miraculously unscrambled my handwriting and fashioned it into neat pages of coherent, crisp type.

John Malcolm Brinnin, who in 1952 and 1953 shared with me much of his time with Dylan, has been just as unstinting in 1981 and 1982 with his encouragement, good judgment and editorial advice.

James Merrill, poet, friend and neighbor, who read the text, gave not only sage advice but made me see how easily an expert could clarify an over-complicated sentence.

Caitlin Thomas, who has remained charmingly loyal since we met in Laugharne, has been generous and trusting in allowing me to use personal material of hers in my possession, without which this book would be the poorer.

Aeron Thomas Ellis, daughter of Dylan and Caitlin, courteously provided me with information about herself and her brothers, Llewelyn and Colm.

Pamela Askew, Professor of Art at Vassar College, who took the jacket photograph of me on my first trip to Laugharne, recently did research for the book in London.

Ann Taylor, my god-daughter, who stole time from a busy painting schedule to travel with me in Southwest Wales last summer, rekindled my spirits and revived my enthusiasm for Dylan's country.

John Ackerman, author of *Welsh Dylan* and other works about the poet, gave Ann and me many clues to parts of Wales, other than Laugharne, important to Dylan. We visited these places in July and I regret that I was not able to incorporate them in this memoir.

Alan Davies, long-time resident of Laugharne and proprietor of Manchester House, where newspapers, books, records and sundries are sold, recognized me after twenty-four years and gave me news of people I had come to know there.

Aeron Owen, writer and photographer, told me much about Laugharne when I saw him there, with his wife Sonya, shortly before he moved to Swansea.

Samina Quraeshi has combined her intelligent sensitivity and professionalism to design this book.

It would never have existed without the tireless energy and perseverance of my publisher, Barbara Holdridge, who recorded Dylan in 1952 and 1953 on the Caedmon label.

Because of these friends I have not had a lonely moment in the creation of *Portrait of Dylan: A Photographer's Memoir.*

Rollie McKenna
Stonington, Connecticut
March 1982

Notes on the Text

p. ii "Invisible, your clocking tides . . ."
From "Where Once the Waters of Your Face," *Collected Poems.*

p. 17 "My own news is very big . . ."
From a 15 July, 1937 letter from *Letters to Vernon Watkins,* by Dylan Thomas, 1957.
"It turned away . . ."
From "Poem in October," *Collected Poems,* by Dylan Thomas.

p. 18 "In my seashaken house . . ."
From "Author's Prologue," *Collected Poems,* by Dylan Thomas.

p. 20 "A Story": "If you can call it a story . . ."
From "A Story," *Quite Early One Morning,* by Dylan Thomas, 1954.

p. 23 "Shall I unbolt or stay . . ."
From "Ears in the Turrets Hear," *Collected Poems,* by Dylan Thomas.

p. 29 "Outside, the sun springs . . ."
Spoken by First Voice in *Under Milk Wood,* by Dylan Thomas, 1954.

p. 30 "And in the town . . ."
Spoken by First Voice in *Under Milk Wood,* by Dylan Thomas, 1954.

p. 31 ". . . where everything is sold . . ."
Spoken by First Voice in *Under Milk Wood,* by Dylan Thomas, 1954.

p. 33 "Hoo, there, in castle keep . . ."
From "Author's Prologue," *Collected Poems,* by Dylan Thomas.

p. 35 "The owls are hunting . . . ."
Spoken by First Voice in *Under Milk Wood,* by Dylan Thomas, 1954.

p. 37 "The ship's clock in the bar . . ."
Spoken by First Voice in *Under Milk Wood,* by Dylan Thomas, 1954.

p. 38 ". . .for a whole year . . ."
Excerpt from a letter dated Laugharne, 16th February 1953, written to Charles Fry about a future book Dylan Thomas was to have written. Courtesy George Firmage.

p. 39 "Over Sir John's hill . . ."
From "Over Sir John's hill," *Collected Poems,* by Dylan Thomas.
"Pale rain over the dwindling harbour"
From "Poem in October," *Collected Poems,* by Dylan Thomas.

p. 40 "These thieves of my love . . ."
From *Leftover Life to Kill,* by Caitlin Thomas, 1957.
". . . so that I can get down . . ."
Excerpt from a letter written to Charles Fry and dated Laugharne, 16 February, 1953. Courtesy George Firmage.

p. 44 "I have longed to move away . . ."
From "I Have Longed to Move Away," *Collected Poems,* by Dylan Thomas.

p. 47 "Ghosts whooed like owls . . ."
From "A Child's Christmas in Wales," *Quite Early One Morning,* by Dylan Thomas, 1954.

p. 49 ". . . tinted photograph of Annie . . ."
From "The Peaches," *Portrait of the Artist as a Young Dog,* by Dylan Thomas, 1940. Second printing 1950.

p. 50 "I stand, for this memorial's sake . . ."
From "After the Funeral," *Collected Poems,* by Dylan Thomas.

p. 53 ". . . it was lovely . . ."
From "Fern Hill," *Collected Poems,* by Dylan Thomas.

p. 55 "Beyond that unknown Wales . . ."
From "Reminiscences of Childhood," *Quite Early One Morning,* by Dylan Thomas, 1954.

p. 56 ". . . immortalized in a moment . . ."
From "Adventures in the Skin Trade," *Adventures in the Skin Trade* and Other Stories, by Dylan Thomas, 1955.
". . . in our first, know-nothing lamb-sappy days"
From *Leftover Life to Kill,* by Caitlin Thomas, **Atlantic - Little, Brown.**

p. 59 "I who was rich . . ."
From "Before I Knocked," *Collected Poems,* by Dylan Thomas.

p. 60 "There are so many petty jobs . . ."
From "Three Letters" from Dylan Thomas to Mme. Caetani, *Botteghe Oscure,* Vol. 13, 1953.
This excerpt and the following ones, "I . . . flew over America . . ." and "looney maybe-play" are from the second letter dated November 6, 1953.

p. 65 "Now I am a man no more . . ."
From "Lament," *Collected Poems,* by Dylan Thomas.

p. 68 "I . . . flew over America . . ."
cf. p. 60.

p. 71 " Love the words . . ."
Author's recollection.
"One moment he was flat out"
From *Leftover Life to Kill,* by Caitlin Thomas, 1957.

p. 72 "To begin at the beginning . . ."
"At the sea end of town . . ."
Spoken by First Voice in *Under Milk Wood,* by Dylan Thomas, 1954.

"But I always think . . ."
Sung by Polly Garter in *Under Milk Wood,* by Dylan Thomas, 1954.

"I saw you talking to a saint . . ."
Spoken by Mrs. Pugh in *Under Milk Wood,* by Dylan Thomas, 1954.

p. 73 "Down in the dusking town . . ."
Spoken by Second Voice in *Under Milk Wood,* by Dylan Thomas, 1954.

p. 74 "Here's your arsenic, dear . . ."
Spoken by Mr. Pugh in *Under Milk Wood,* by Dylan Thomas, 1954.

p. 75 "I'm *fast.* I'm a bad lot . . . ."
Spoken by Mae Rose Cottage in *Under Milk Wood,* by Dylan Thomas, 1954.
"I am a draper . . ."
Spoken by Mr. Edwards in *Under Milk Wood,* by Dylan Thomas, 1954.

p. 76 Five performers and Dylan, taking fifty-four parts
The number of parts went through several changes before this performance and the New Directions publication of *Under Milk Wood* in 1954.

p. 78 "I learned of Dylan's last day in London . . ."
This excerpt from John Malcolm Brinnin's personal journal is printed with his kind permission. Philip Burton is the foster-father of actor Richard Burton.

p. 79 "I've had eighteen straight whiskies . . ."
From *Dylan Thomas in America,* by John Malcolm Brinnin, 1955.

p. 83 ". . . a few gnawing bafflements"
From a letter dated December 15, 1953. This quotation and those which follow, as well as the cartoons, are part of the author's private collection and are used with the generous permission of Caitlin Thomas.
"At poor peace . . ."
From "Author's Prologue," *Collected Poems,* by Dylan Thomas.

"I, born of flesh . . ."
From "Before I Knocked," *Collected Poems,* by Dylan Thomas.

p. 84 "Years and years and years ago . . ."
From "A Child's Christmas in Wales," *Quite Early One Morning,* by Dylan Thomas, 1954.
"A Child's Christmas in Wales" was first published in *Harper's Bazaar* about 1945 and was revised in 1950.
". . . And the park itself was a world . . ."
From "Reminiscences of Childhood," *Quite Early One Morning,* by Dylan Thomas, 1954.
The photograph is of Number 5 Cwmdonkin Drive, where Dylan was born and lived with his mother and father. It was here as well as in the countryside that—as a young adolescent—he developed many of his favorite images of Wales.

p. 86 "NARRATOR We had reached the last gate . . ."
From "Return Journey," *Quite Early One Morning,* by Dylan Thomas, 1954.
"The hunchback in the park"
From poem of the same title, *Collected Poems,* by Dylan Thomas.

p. 87 ". . . And the park itself was a world"
cf. p. 84.

p. 88 "I was born in a large Welsh town . . ."
From "Reminiscences of Childhood," *Quite Early One Morning,* by Dylan Thomas, New Directions.

p. 93 "Hark, I trumpet the place . . ."
From "Author's Prologue," *Collected Poems,* by Dylan Thomas, lines 17-20.
". . . We pointed out to each other"
From "Who Do You Wish Was With Us," *Portrait of the Artist as a Young Dog,* by Dylan Thomas, 1940. Second printing 1950. (Quotations from this one through the sentence beginning, "On the mainland, in the dusk . . . ," are excerpted from this story.)

p. 95 "He can't swim . . ."
From "Extraordinary Little Cough," *Portrait of the Artist as a Young Dog,* by Dylan Thomas, 1940. Second printing, 1950. (Quotations through "I've been running and running" are from this story.)

p. 97 "I've been running and running. . ."
cf. p. 95.

p. 98 "The dream has sucked . . ."
From "Our Eunuch Dreams," *Collected Poems,* by Dylan Thomas, New Directions.

p. 100 "Dylan and dying . . ."
From *Leftover Life to Kill,* by Caitlin Thomas, 1957.

p. 105 "And all the people . . ."
Read by First Voice in *Under Milk Wood,* by Dylan Thomas, 1954.

Designed by Samina Quraeshi

Composed in Baskerville by
Service Composition Company, Baltimore, Maryland

Color separations, jacket and text printing
by Wolk Press, Inc., Woodlawn, Maryland, on 100 lb. Black and White enamel

Bound in Holliston Crown Linen cloth by Delmar Printing Company,
Charlotte, North Carolina